You may not reproduce, duplicate or send the contents of this book witout direct written permission from the author. You cannot hereby despite any circumstance blame the publisher or hold him or her to legal responsibility for any reparation, compensation, or monetary forfeiture owing to the information included herein, either in a direct or an indirect way.

legal Notice: This book has copyright protection. You can use the book for personal purpose. You should not sell, use , ulter, distribute, quote, take excerpts or paraphrase in part or whole the material conained in this book without obtaining the permission of the author first.

Disclaimer Notice: You must take note that the information in this document is for casual reading and entertainment purposes only.
We have made every attempt to provide accurate, up to date and reliable information. We do not express or imply guarantees of any kind. The persons who read admit that the writer is not occupied in giving legal, financial, medical or other advice. We put this book content by sourcing various places.

please consult a liecensed professional before you try any techniques shown in this book. by going through this document, the book lover comes to an agreement that under no situation is the author accountable for any forfeiture, direct or indirect, which they may incur because of the use of material contained in this document, including, but not limited to, -- errors, omissions, or inaccuracies.

Practice Lines

STEP 1

Cute Out the sheet using trim line

STEP 2

Color the picture

STEP 3

Cut out the picture using the guide line carefuly

STEP 4

pas te it on another sheet or hang it

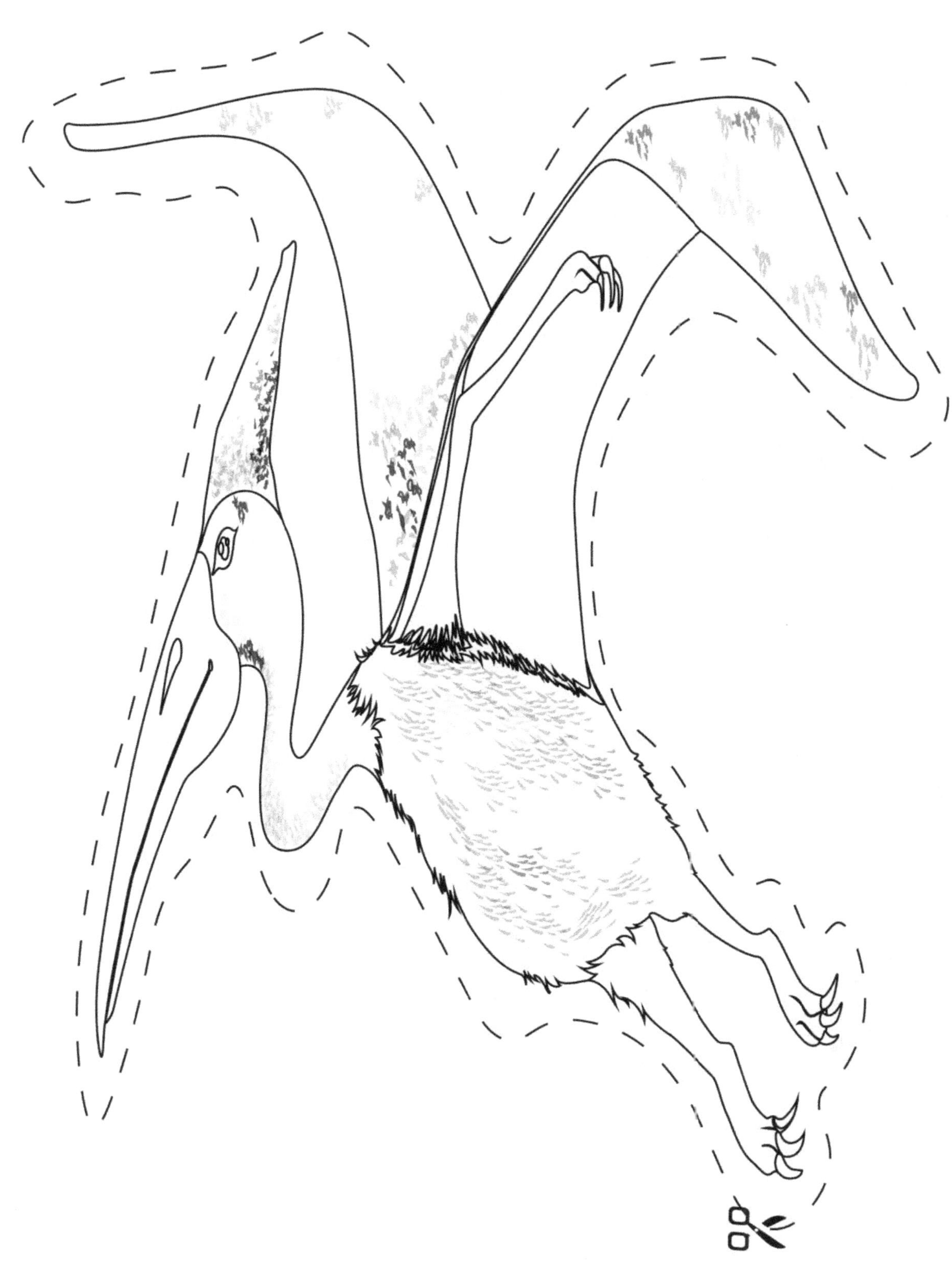

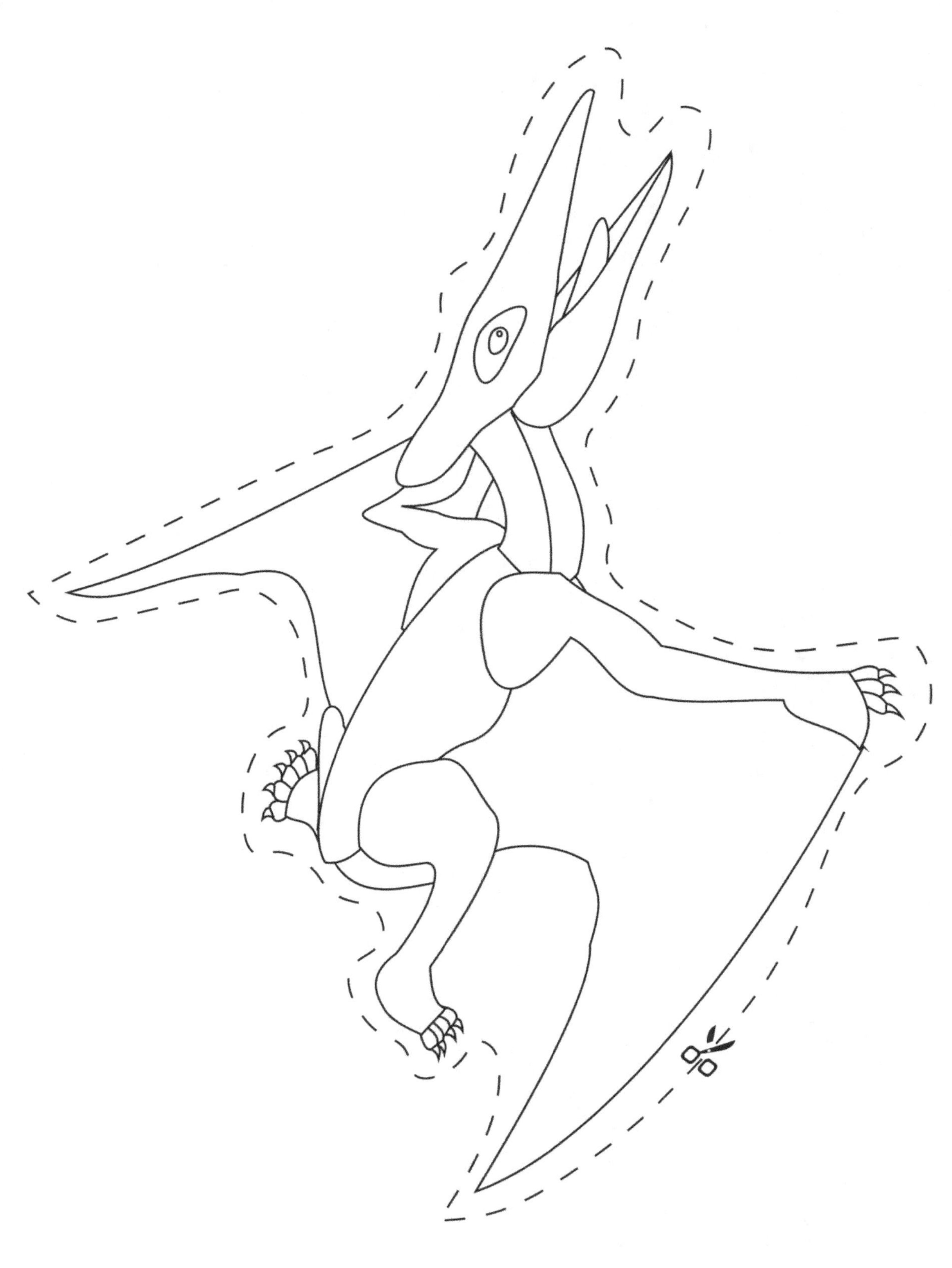

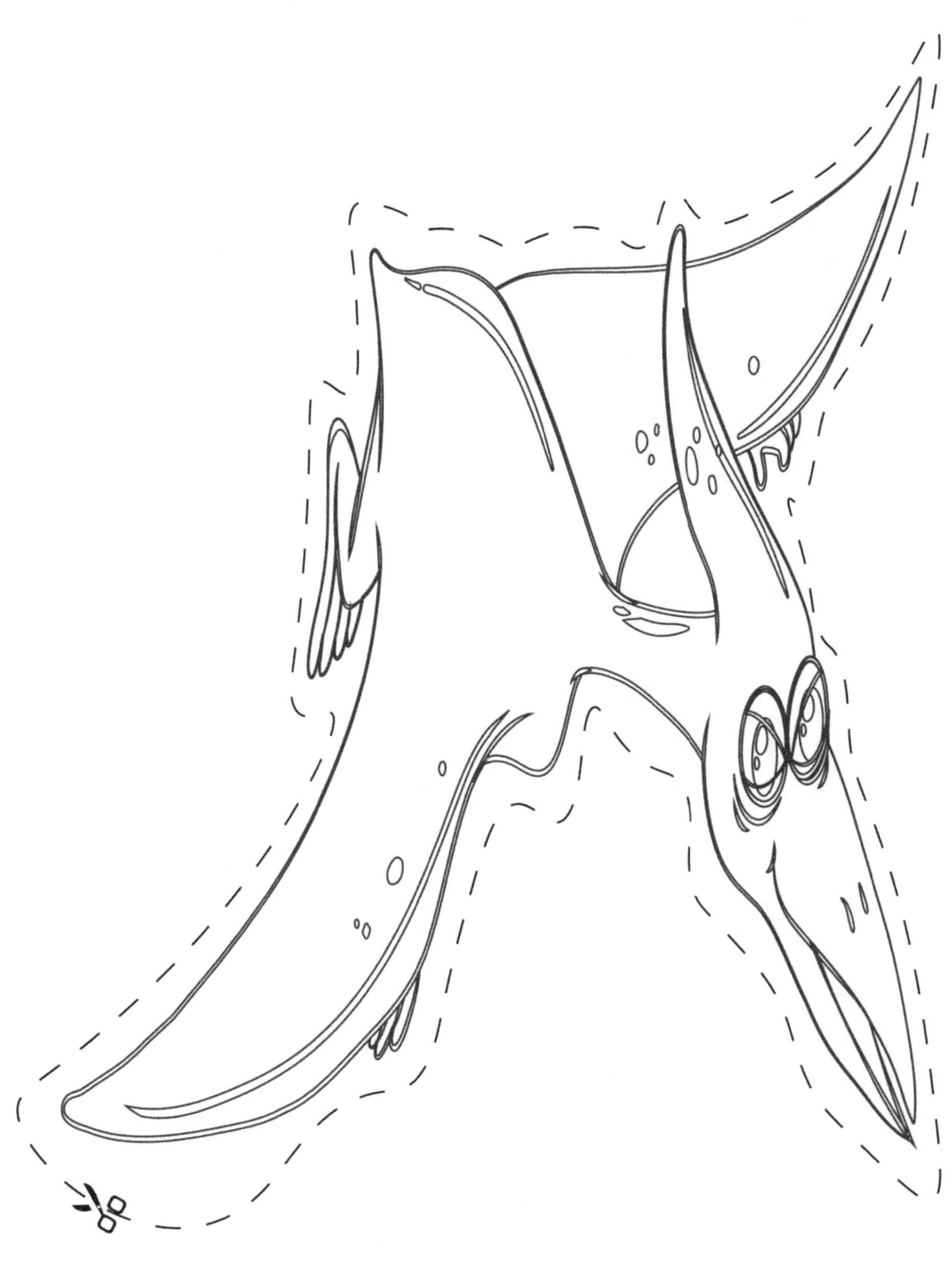